A Single European Currency?

A Single European Currency?

Jeffrey Gedmin, editor

The AEI Press

Publisher for the American Enterprise Institute
WASHINGTON, D.C.
1997

Available in the United States from the AEI Press, c/o Publisher Resources, Inc., 1224 Heil Quaker Blvd., P.O. Box 7001, La Vergne, TN 37086-7001. Distributed outside the United States by arrangement with Eurospan, 3 Henrietta Street, London WC2E 8LU England.

ISBN 0-8447-7097-3

1 3 5 7 9 10 8 6 4 2

THE AEI PRESS
Publisher for the American Enterprise Institute
1150 17th Street, N.W., Washington, D.C. 20036

Printed in the United States of America

Contents

v

CONTENTS

Preface

*"Europe is first and foremost a political program, not an
economic program."*

Wolfgang Schäuble
Chairman, German Christian Democratic Union

*"Without economic and monetary union, there will be no
political union."*

Helmut Kohl
Chancellor of Germany

In 1987, three decades after the European Community
was launched by the Treaty of Rome, Western European governments introduced the Single European Act.
The measure cleared the way for a more developed single
market. But while the act was considered chiefly a com-
mercial arrangement, it also represented a further amal-
gamation of the national sovereignties of member states.

Five years later, the Treaty on European Union, initialed
in the Dutch city of Maastricht, advanced the course of deep-
ening European integration by charting an explicit course
for monetary union. Jacques Delors, president of the European Commission until 1994, readily professed the political nature of the project. For Delors, monetary union
was a key to the political unification of Europe. And European unity, in Delors's thinking, was an essential means by
which to extend French influence, to tame the power of a
unified Germany, and to compete with the economic power
and political clout of the United States and Japan. In German Chancellor Kohl's view, monetary union and the trans-

fer of economic and political power from national governments to supranational institutions would provide the greatest security against reemergent nationalism and the prospect of war on the continent. If achieved, monetary union and political union would likely constitute the greatest voluntary transfer of sovereignty in history.

In recent months the debate over the political *and* economic consequences of a single European currency has intensified. How will relations develop between countries included and those excluded from monetary union? How will monetary union affect the ambitions of central European countries to join the EU? What effect is a single European currency likely to have on interest rates, unemployment, and the international trading order?

In September 1996, the New Atlantic Initiative convened a panel of three leading economic observers at the American Enterprise Institute (AEI) in Washington, D.C., to discuss the efficacy and outcome of the EU's efforts to adopt a single currency. Allan Meltzer is a resident scholar at AEI and professor of economics at Carnegie Mellon University in Pittsburgh. Paul Mentré is executive secretary of the Committee for the Monetary Union of Europe. Otmar Issing is a member of the Directorate of the German Bundesbank. Their presentations are published here along with an incisive and compelling commentary by Czech Prime Minister Václav Klaus, who delivered the session's luncheon address. The conference was open to the public and was attended by approximately 200 guests, including government officials, scholars, journalists, and business executives.

JEFFREY GEDMIN

Contributors

JEFFREY GEDMIN is executive director of the New Atlantic Initiative and a research fellow at the American Enterprise Institute, writing and lecturing on German and European politics and U.S.–European relations. He is the author of *The Hidden Hand: Gorbachev and the Collapse of East Germany* and editor of *European Integration and American Interests: What the New Europe Really Means for the United States.* Mr. Gedmin was the executive director and producer of the 1995 PBS television documentary *The Germans: Portrait of a New Nation.*

OTMAR ISSING is a member of the Directorate of the Deutsche Bundesbank. He is a member of the Central Bank Council, the Academy of Sciences and Literature in Mainz, and the German Council of Scientific Experts. He was a member of the advisory council of the German Federal Ministry of Economics from 1980 to 1990. He is the author of *Introduction to Monetary Policy* and of *Introduction to Monetary Theory.*

VÁCLAV KLAUS, once a dissident economist in Communist Czechoslovakia, has been prime minister of the Czech Republic since 1992. He is the leader of the Civic Democratic Party and an eloquent advocate of democracy, free markets, NATO expansion, and strong transatlantic relations. Mr. Klaus's extraordinary leadership is widely credited for the Czech Republic's remarkable success, notably: the velvet divorce between the Czech Republic and Slovakia; a stable, democratic government; and a market-oriented economic transformation. He is the recipient of numerous awards, including the International Freedom Foundation's Freedom Award and the Konrad Adenauer Prize.

ALLAN H. MELTZER is a visiting scholar at the American Enterprise Institute and is University Professor of Political Economy and Public Policy at Carnegie Mellon University. He is the honorary adviser to the Institute for Monetary and Economic Studies of the Bank of Japan. Mr. Meltzer was a member of the President's Economic Policy Advisory Board during the Reagan administration. He has been an acting member of the President's Council of Economic Advisers and a consultant to the U.S. Treasury and to the Board of Governors of the Federal Reserve System. He is the author of several books and more than 200 papers on economic theory and policy. Mr. Meltzer is a founder and chairman of the Shadow Open Market Committee, which issues policy statements about current events to government agencies and to the public.

PAUL MENTRÉ is the executive secretary of the Committee for the Monetary Union of Europe, and he is inspecteur général des finances. He was the financial minister for the French embassy in Washington, D.C., from 1978 to 1982 and was the executive director of the IMF and the World Bank from 1978 to 1981. From 1982 to 1986, he was the chairman and CEO of the Crédit National. He is the author of many articles and books on economics, the most recent of which is *L'insoutenable légèreté du fort*.

1

European Monetary Union and Its Systemic and Fiscal Consequences

Václav Klaus

European Monetary Union—as a distinct political, and therefore not only purely economic project—has at present become one of the dominant political goals of the European integration process. It is a political goal of politicians rather than a goal of citizens of European countries, but because we live in the era of *indirect, representative* democracy, the difference is not so important. The decision to create the European Monetary Union is the most important one taken since the end of World War II. Despite this fact, I cannot resist the impression that the problems regarding the European Monetary Union—because it is predominantly a political endeavor—are being trivialized. We overestimate its advantages and ignore or fully omit its disadvantages.

The main advantage is the possibility of moving within one monetary area without having to exchange money every hundred kilometers, without being victims of unexpected devaluations or revaluations. But nothing is free, and our main task is to find out whether the benefits of the monetary integration will prevail over the costs.

These are not minor considerations, the concerns of a "Europessimist." These are the issues voiced by a responsible politician who has spent the majority of his life in a Communist regime, where the basic structural characteristics were not central planning or state ownership, not even the dominant role of the Communist Party, but rather the priority of politics before economics. The Communist regime embraced the idea that it is possible for politics to dictate economics.

These are the concerns of a politician who knows that European integration is our common future; of a politician who tries to make sure that the result is the best result possible. Additionally, these are the concerns of a politician who expects that his country will become a full member of the European Union in the near future, and it will not wish to play an outsider's role there.

From the theoretical point of view, it is important to ask whether today's Europe is an "optimal currency area" (according to a definition by Mundell from 1961), and if it is not, whether the ex ante organized monetary unification will help to create such an area and at what cost.

There is no doubt that the European Union is still characterized by a very heterogeneous structure of its member countries and that today's fifteen-member European Union is not an optimal currency area. This heterogeneity is not an obstacle to lower forms of economic integration (such as the common market or customs union), but it is an obstacle to the emergence and smooth functioning of the monetary union—as we could learn from the collapse of the Czechoslovak monetary union and from the politically motivated quick monetary union of Germany. If we look at history, we could speculate about whether or not the monetary union of Italy in 1861 helped to "freeze" the economic *imbalance* between the Italian north and south. At the same time, a certain homogenization process exists, thanks to intentional political-economic measures. The original European "six" are definitely more homogeneous than today's "fifteen" or the future's "twenty" or "twenty-seven."

What are the reasons for the present heterogeneity of the economic structure of today's Europe? What will be its consequences for the future monetary union, and what could minimize its negative effects?

Economic Heterogeneity

There are several reasons for the heterogeneity of the economic structure of today's Europe. First, there are natural differences in the endowment of the individual countries with factors of production, including such variables as weather, natural resources, and access to the sea. Because of these differences, the effects of the exogenous changes, or external shocks, are different in various economies. The existing differences cannot be underestimated. Their existence is documented daily by the nonnegligible tensions inside some countries of the European Union—for example, in the north and south of Italy. And this happens despite the fact that there is an undoubtedly stronger feeling of solidarity in these countries than there will be among countries in the future monetary union. This problem does not have the slightest connection with accomplishing the so-called Maastricht criteria.

Second, in Europe, there are very different "national propensities," traditions and habits that can hardly be changed, considering their long-term historical anchoring. Alternatively, their change in short- or middle-term anchoring is not possible—it is not certain that it is desirable. We could name a large number of examples of such national peculiarities, and the existing differences between countries will naturally be a source of future problems. Therefore, it can be predicted that the conflict concerning the extent and duration of transfers from rich to poor countries and from rapidly developing to stagnating ones will be one of the permanent characteristics of the monetary union.

The third reason for heterogeneity is something that would be possible to change, but that is in every moment "given"—like the weather or the supply of gas. I speak of the prevailing ideology and the resulting economic policies of a choice between the conflicting goals and of a choice of the instrumentarium of economic policy. Europe is not homogeneous; there has not been any "end of ideology," as predicted by Fukuyama. There are countries with right-of-center or left-of-center governments, and political fights inside any country are irreconcilable, as always. The dreams of some European politicians that these problems will die and that some nonpolitical or suprapolitical rationality will prevail are an example of one very concrete and very well-known ideology. It is an ideology that I do not share. Priorities and preferences of various countries differ today and will differ in the future.

Consequences of the Future Monetary Union

Introducing a single currency or transferring one economic parameter from the category of variables to the category of constants will mean three things.

First, there will be unequal effects from world trade and its fluctuations (but also from other exogenous influences) on various countries without the chance of short-term and middle-term adjustments in nominal variables. Maastricht convergence criteria do not include the economic growth or the dynamics of output, wages, and employment. These variables will grow in various countries quite differently. This different development will not lead to changes in the exchange rate.

Second, the political unacceptability of growing differences in the economic level among countries will bring about the increase of transfer payments among countries and the centralization of budgets into the center of the European Union. The solidaristic character of the Union will grow, and the autonomy of fiscal policies and of decision-making authority will diminish. Some of us may want this, some not. But we cannot pretend that such a problem does not exist.

VÁCLAV KLAUS

Third, the shift in decision-making structures will bring about a shift in the structure of basic political and constitutional institutions, and it will mean a visible ideological change from a traditional liberal (contractual) society to a more constructivist (and political) system. It is being discussed in Europe these days under the heading "democratic deficit."

Minimizing the Impact

Minimizing the negative effects of the introduction of monetary union to a nonhomogeneous area depends on two issues: the degree of flexibility of the factors of production and of their prices, and the degree of authentic European solidarity.

The monetary union will be easier to form if the degree of mobility of the basic factors of production, labor plus capital, is higher—even though there is no symmetry. "Greater labour mobility is a cementing force of the union, while greater capital mobility is not," P. Bolton et al., *Economic Theories of the Breakup and Integration of Nations* (Brussels, ECARE, September 1995). The mobility of labor in Europe, as compared with America, is low, and if I am not mistaken, no one in Europe is interested in its growth at present. None of us wishes for "voting by feet," which means that a less successful country would be getting depopulated, and vice versa. If such a process is not to take place, there must be either an idyllic epoch of an absolutely balanced, harmonic economic growth or an artificial coverage of differences by financial transfers from more successful toward less successful countries. (Growing mobility of capital means that this problem is becoming more serious, because capital follows success, not vice versa.)

The same is true about price flexibility. The monetary union will be the more difficult to organize, the more rigid the prices of factors of production. The price of labor is traditionally very rigid, and I do not see any real chance to

5

weaken the existing downward wage rigidity. Again, significant fiscal transfers will have to follow.

Again and again there is a question of fiscal transfers and European solidarity. The so-called cohesion fund founded by the Maastricht Treaty represents an elementary form of the future European fiscal mechanism—the only difference being that it will be more costly. Every politician knows that a 1 percent increase or reduction in the share of state budget on GDP inside a country leads to the occasional fall of a government or to a change in election results. The idea that European taxes and European transfer payments will be excluded and put "in front of the brackets," that they will not be politically disputed, that they will stay away from standard political battles, seems to me quite unrealistic. The relationship between the individual and the state, along with any above-individual structure, is a basis of political discussion in every democratic society and must not be changed in the future Europe. As a politician, I would like to decide on something "in front of the brackets"; as a citizen, I wish to minimize such decisions.

I began by saying that I consider the European Monetary Union the biggest postwar change, including the collapse of communism in the eastern part of Europe. We have to discuss this issue seriously—not only the ultimate solution, but also the problems of transition from one system to another. I hope that the debate about this will continue.

2

A German Perspective on Monetary Union

Otmar Issing

Contrary to what you might have heard, the Bundesbank is not opposed to European Monetary Union, which in the end means abandoning the deutsche mark as Germany's currency. As a German central banker, I am a member of an endangered species. We are investing tremendous effort in the preparation for European Monetary Union (EMU), but we are convinced that only a stable Europe can fulfill the high expectations it has created. Therefore we never cease stressing that the conditions for entry must be strictly fulfilled. We take the Maastricht Treaty seriously.

Historical experience shows that national territories and monetary territories normally coincide. In the age of paper currencies, the relevant legislation, as a rule, defines monetary sovereignty in relation to a national territory. Monetary policy is considered to be so important that no state will renounce these sovereign rights without compelling reasons.

Monetary Union and Political Integration

In contrast with the normal rule, the Maastricht Treaty implies a clear discrepancy between monetary and political integration. For those member states qualifying for the European Monetary Union, the ultimate goal is unrestricted participation in a common monetary system and a single currency, whereas great steps toward political union are rather modest. Even the concrete form of the goal as such remains weak. This is not necessarily regarded as a problem by politicians. Among politicians, there is a widespread view that the introduction of common money will trigger a process that will inevitably lead to international unity. Jacques Rueff, for example, put this view in a nutshell as early as 1950, saying, "L'Europe se fera par la monnaie ou ne se fera pas"—either it will happen that Europe will construct itself through its currency, or it just won't happen.

From an economist's point of view, there are no convincing reasons to expect that the desired form of political integration will automatically come about with premature entry into monetary union. Agreeing on a single currency is itself an important step, and moreover, it creates constraints on other areas of policy. This will not suffice, however, to advance the desired political integration decisively if the political will is not strong enough to endorse this goal openly and to accept the inescapable restrictions of political action. A Europe that ventures the transition to monetary union ultimately cannot avoid making a decision on the shape of the political union.

From today's perspective, however, it is to be expected that the discrepancy between monetary and political integration built into the Maastricht Treaty will persist for the foreseeable future. The continuing intergovernmental conference is unlikely to change that substantially. If this prognosis is correct, the discrepancy will give rise to the following consequences.

First, the Maastricht Treaty demands of the member countries a process of convergence toward stability on the basis of low rates of inflation. Second, it promises sustained price stability for the period after entry into monetary union. In other words, the promise that the Euro will be a stable currency is the foundation of the entire project.

By providing for the independence of the European

Central Bank (ECB) and stipulating the priority of the objective of price stability, the statute of the ECB creates crucial institutional preconditions for monetary policy makers being able to achieve the expectations invested in them. We know from experience, however, that the central bank is overtaxed by the task of keeping the value of money stable if wage trends get out of hand and fiscal policy makers pursue an unsound course. It is, therefore, important to protect the future European Central Bank's monetary policy as far as possible against these potential dangers.

Difficulties for Wage Policy Makers

The difficulties with which wage policy makers will be confronted in the monetary union should not be underrated. As the "exchange rate illusion" will no longer exist, wage differences will become more transparent; judging by past experience, this will trigger a pressure to adjust wages. Without impairing growth, employment, and monetary stability, it will be possible to level off wage differences only if productivity increases differ accordingly. Early success is not to be expected. As detrimental as an enforced wage adjustment would be— the Europeanization of wage policy, in a sense—uniform pay-rate increases are agreed on within the common currency area. Such increases would not only lock in existing wage differences; they would also preclude from the outset a differentiated response to the concrete labor market situation of the respective sector or region.

Calls to supplement monetary union with a social union are likewise on the wrong track. Social union in the European debate essentially means a harmonization of social standards—what is more, at the highest possible level. Social union demands a greater number of and more stringent regulations of the labor market. Monetary union requires the opposite: considerably more flexibility in the labor market.

In order to safeguard price stability, the union must

provide permanent protection against potentially undesirable developments in public finance. The inherent logic of the Maastricht Treaty calls for appropriate arrangements to be made concerning the fiscal policy of the member states within the monetary union. This follows from the asymmetry in the treaty. Any country not fulfilling the two fiscal policy criteria—for the budget deficit and public indebtedness—in stage two is subjected to the toughest conceivable sanction: it is barred from entry. Any country that has already been admitted to the monetary union is exposed, in the event of fiscal slippage, only to the comparatively mild deterrent of the excessive deficit procedure pursuant to Article 104(c).

Monetary union may reduce a government's incentive to conduct a prudent fiscal policy, because under a single currency there is no national exchange rate, and upward pressure on interest rates caused by higher national budget deficits is reduced in the single capital market. The partner countries will have to share the adverse consequences of an undesirable fiscal-policy stance of a member state, in the form of higher interest rates. Without appropriate safeguards, the capital market of a single currency must create an incentive to build up deficits; that is, it produces moral hazard.

Reference to the "no bailout" clause of the Maastricht Treaty provides little comfort in this context, I think. Suppose, for example, that a member state in the community is exposed if necessary to the sanction of bankruptcy. Will the markets really believe in the effectiveness of the "no bailout" clause and penalize the state that incurs excessive debt with a rising risk threat to its interest rate, and would this stop a state at an early stage of such fiscal imprudence?

It is often claimed that the flexibility of national fiscal policies must not be restricted in a regime of irrevocably fixed exchange rates. Statutory restrictions limiting the scope for fiscal policy action are said to be counterproductive in a recession and could, in the worst case, even jeop-

ardize the continued existence of the union. This line of
reasoning suffers from a misconception about the characteristics of appropriate safeguards. If, for instance, the 3
percent criterion for the budget deficit were prescribed as
a statutory upper limit for national governments having
joined the monetary union, the authorities in each country would be responsible for ensuring the necessary lee-
way. In buoyant economic conditions, the budget deficit
would thus have to be much lower in order to provide fiscal policy makers with the appropriate scope for running
up higher deficits in periods of recession.

There is no need for a large European Community budget to smooth business cycles. Unless the union is assigned
tasks that require considerable financial resources, there is
no convincing argument for raising the Community budget. Enduring the flexibility needed for responding to cy-
clical trends by pursuing an appropriate fiscal policy will
remain the responsibility of national parliaments and governments.

The risk that fiscal policy will cause tensions in the monetary union is all the greater the more "generously" the
fiscal policy convergence criteria are interpreted before entry. If, even under the threat of exclusion, a member state
is neither willing nor able to observe the limits for the budget deficit and indebtedness, it is hardly likely to make increased efforts when such a strict sanction is no longer
available.

The Proposed Stability Pact

Making sound behavior a precondition for entry is rooted
in the perception that countries, too, display certain typi-
cal patterns of behavior. Countries relying on stability within
the monetary union should prove in advance that they are
capable of ensuring fiscal discipline—with the approval of
their citizens, who have placed their trust in the government for precisely that purpose in elections.

11

The lopsided architecture of the Maastricht Treaty requires effective constraints on fiscal policy at the constitutional level—a challenge with which virtually all industrial nations are faced. The states of the European Union should, therefore, view the constraints resulting from the logic of the Maastricht process as an opportunity to do collectively what every country itself would sooner or later have to tackle in its own national interests anyway.

The so-called stability pact proposed by the German finance minister is a very promising approach and deserves support. In implementing a stability pact with clear rules, including automatic sanctions in the case of misbehavior, the member states could give a convincing signal to the financial markets if monetary union is to be built on a sure foundation and can fulfill the great expectations that are associated with this project.

3

An American Perspective on Monetary Union

Allan H. Meltzer

Recently, a European banker complained that U.S. bankers and the public know more about emu, the Australian, ostrich-like bird, than about EMU, the European Monetary Union. On this side of the Atlantic, EMU is almost a nonevent. In contrast, monetary union is a major event for Europe's bankers and political classes. There are frequent meetings to work out the technical details and resolve the remaining political ambiguities. There is endless talk about which countries will be in, which will be out, how the ins will maintain relations with the outs, and a host of other issues.

My impression, based only on personal questioning, is that the ordinary European knows a bit more than his U.S. counterpart, but not a lot more. He or she may know that the currency is going to change, but is not entirely clear about what that means or when it will happen. There is, however, appropriate skepticism about the benefits claimed by political leaders and considerable doubt as to exactly what the fuss is all about.

European Skepticism about EMU

With unemployment rates between 10 and 20 percent, with most of the unemployment persistent and long-term, with recession or stagnation common to many of the countries, with theft and burglary at record levels, and with many other

13

social and economic problems unresolved, there is also massive uncertainty about why political leaders pay so much attention to monetary union. The European public is right to be querulous and questioning. The case for monetary union is weak. It is, at best, uncertain whether monetary union will make a net positive contribution to the stability of Europe and to renewed growth of the European economy.

The potential of monetary union for good or ill ranks far below such issues as the integration of Central and Eastern Europe into a harmonious European Union, the revamping of the excessive economic burdens of social welfare states, the reform of agricultural policies to permit freer trade within Europe and particularly between Eastern and Western Europe, and, as the Bosnian fiasco illuminated, the ability of Europeans to prevent or stop religious, ethnic, or tribal wars in Europe.

Among the problems that European leaders face, monetary union seems to have little possibility of bringing major advance, but considerable risk for causing serious harm.

The plan for monetary union calls for the nations that join to replace their own currencies in a series of steps with a common currency and monetary unit called the Euro. Beginning in January 1999, each of the participating countries will fix its exchange rate irrevocably against the Euro. Old currencies, such as francs, guilders, and marks, will continue in use but will exist only as units of the new Euro currency.

The old central banks will no longer conduct monetary policy. A European Central Bank, similar to the Federal Reserve's Open Market Committee, will set an interest rate or money growth target and will be responsible for maintaining price stability in the member countries.

Between 1999 and 2002, a series of steps will increase the role of the Euro in trade and finance. In 2002, the Euro currency and coins will replace existing currencies, and the formal transition will be complete in the member countries. The Euro, like the dollar, will have a fixed exchange rate internally and a fluctuating exchange rate against other major currencies.

Transaction costs for converting or exchanging currencies and exchange rate instability will be eliminated for all transactions within the monetary union, just as they are in the United States. Proponents of monetary union often draw verbal pictures of the benefits that have accrued to the United States from a large common market with a common currency and no barriers in trade or asset markets.

Monetary Union and Political Stability

No one who is dimly aware of European history since 1815 or 1870 can doubt the importance of institutional changes that would make improbable another European war or another war between France and Germany. The past fifty years of German and French policies have had no more important goal or overriding objective than avoidance of another war.

Proponents of monetary union, when pressed about the modest size of the economic benefits, typically fall back to a political argument. Chancellor Helmut Kohl, a tireless and arguably the leading advocate of monetary union, leaves little doubt that the alleged economic benefits are the least important benefits.

The monetary union is, at heart, an economic union intended to achieve a political goal, binding France to Germany and Germany to France. The proposed chains are monetary, not because they are the most effective or the most appropriate; they are not. They have been chosen because Europe, or even Germany and France, are unwilling to mention political union or federation as a feasible near-term prospect. One need only look at the impotent European parliament at Strasbourg to see how little power has been ceded to quasi-representative federal institutions.

To an outsider, the obvious road to European union

15

should go through Strasbourg, where a European parliament meets, elected by Europe's voters. By gradually expanding the parliament's role with voter approval, a European Union would begin to provide common goods, such as defense, foreign policy, air pollution control, rules for trade and asset transfers, rules for migration of labor and capital, and even limited powers to tax citizens of the union.

A union of this kind could claim to be based on the consent of the governed. Its powers and legitimacy would be derived, at least indirectly, from the voters, and the voters would be able to express their satisfaction or dissatisfaction with what parliament had done or failed to do.

The union that has been proposed is a very unconventional structure. It is not an independent central bank within government, as is the Federal Reserve. The European Central Bank exists outside any government. Its members are appointed by governments for long terms. Ministers of finance or heads of government may whisper in the ears of central bank governors or they may shout, but the governors are not obliged to listen.

The bank's goal is fixed by statute to maintain price stability without qualifications. In practice, the bank may take account of economic conditions within the member countries, but it is not obliged to do so. By law, it may not finance government budget deficits.

This is at once a strength and a weakness. The bank will be able to pursue price stability without political interference, but inevitably, it will be blamed by governments for unemployment and the continued sluggishness of most European economies. After 1999, it will be tempting to blame outsiders, particularly the European Central Bank, for domestic problems. Because monetary union has had little public support or input, it will not have a sizable constituency that supports its objective.

The case for monetary union as an important step toward political stability in Europe has a critical flaw. The

United States had a single currency when the Civil War started. So did Spain, Lebanon, and most recently, Yugoslavia when they fought civil wars. A common currency is neither necessary nor sufficient to prevent war or political disturbances. The ties that bind France and Germany will have to be much stronger than partnership in the printing presses, and, I believe, competent observers would judge that they now are.

An Arranged Marriage

The European Monetary Union is an arranged marriage between France and Germany. The marriage has been arranged at the highest political level. The parties are not the best of friends, but they need each other to accomplish other objectives, some openly confessed, some concealed.

Two of the common objectives are to prevent future political conflict and to fix exchange rates. Germany would like to avoid further appreciation of the deutsche mark against virtually all the European currencies, particularly the French franc. France wants to prevent competitive devaluations by some of its European neighbors, particularly Italy and Spain, and to avoid the sense of humiliation from repeated depreciations against the deutsche mark.

Both Germany and France have other objectives that are not discussed directly. Each wants to improve the partner's conduct after the marriage. Germany wants assurance that France will not return to its profligate ways. They intend their partner to retain the zeal for low inflation and greater fiscal prudence that France lost about the time of World War I, and with the brief exception of the late 1920s and early 1930s rediscovered only in the past ten years.

The French, on their side, want a bigger voice in the choice of monetary policy, and they dare to hope that they can teach the Germans and their other partners to be a bit more moderate and relaxed about inflation than is the current Bundesbank.

Each of the partners brings along some junior partners. The Benelux countries and Austria are small economies in the German orbit. They have no prospect of operating an independent central bank or conducting monetary policy that is independent of Germany's. Those, like Belgium, that tried in the past paid a price to restore stability. Monetary union gives them a small voice in policy formation, but it is a larger voice than they now have.

France would like to have Spain and Italy as partners to prevent these countries from devaluing to reduce unemployment when their exchange rates are misaligned. Both countries would like to join, and France would like their voices and votes at the meeting to weaken the influence of the German bloc.

Spain will pass scrutiny more easily than Italy. Supporting the Italian lira against a possible run during the transition period to a single money has no appeal either to the German government or to the voters, and Italian fiscal spending and future deficits to pay future pensions remain extraordinary even after the recent reform.

To return to the metaphor, a marriage or union that starts with the expectation that one's partner can be reformed usually ends with disappointment, or simply ends. If the only objectives of the union were to have a single currency, that goal could be achieved at much lower economic cost by taking the deutsche mark as the common currency. That would avoid all the costs of adjusting to a new currency with new rules and a new policy-making structure and uncertainty about the outlook for inflation and exchange rates against nonmembers. It would eliminate the concern of holders of long-term German bonds, who will receive payment in Euros, a currency of uncertain value.

Of course, this is out of the question, for political reasons. France and others would view that outcome as German hegemony, not European integration. Raising this alternative makes clear again that the Euro is mainly a solution to a political problem, of making the marriage look like a union of equals and giving France at least the appearance of an equal voice in policy. The economic problems of monetary union are severe. The members of the union get the benefit of a fixed exchange rate, but they lose the opportunity to adjust to real disturbances by devaluing. Devaluation is not a panacea, but at times, it is a useful tool. One of those times is when a country's wages or prices are misaligned. An oil shock, German unification, changes in relative productivity, significant new inventions, differences in regulation are only a few of the ways in which countries' costs and prices change relative to costs and prices abroad. These and other real disturbances cause some countries to expand more rapidly, while others contract.

There are only three ways in which countries can adjust. People can move labor and capital from the contracting to the expanding countries. Following the oil shocks of the 1970s, people moved from Michigan and the Midwest to Texas and the Southwest as U.S. auto production slowed and oil production rose. This solution faces language and cultural barriers in Europe. Mobility is often low within countries, as Dr. Klaus mentioned earlier. For all but menial jobs, mobility is almost nonexistent in Europe.

A second solution is to force wages and prices to fall in the contracting country relative to prices in the expanding country. For Europe, high minimum wages and welfare benefits severely restrict this means of adjustment. If a single currency would force Europeans to reduce these and other welfare programs, the indirect benefits for Europe would be larger than the direct benefits. There is little evidence to suggest that such changes are likely, and much to suggest the opposite.

The third means of adjustment is devaluation or revaluation to reduce export prices and production costs in the contracting country and to raise them in the expanding country. Monetary union sacrifices this mechanism without introducing a substitute. For Europe, fixed exchange rates and the welfare state have brought high unemployment and sluggish growth. Monetary union continues along this path.

The benefits of monetary union depend on the number of members and the trade between them. The reason is that the benefits of exchange rate stability apply to trade with other members. If all fifteen countries in the European Union join the monetary union, from 50 to 75 percent of trade would take place at fixed exchange rates. There would be exchange rate stability over the bulk of trade.

If monetary union, however, includes only France, Germany, Austria, the Benelux countries, and Ireland, then two-thirds of German and French trade would be with other nonmembers. The advantages of the union would be small.

Further, members of the European Union that do not join the monetary union would retain devaluation as a means of adjustment to disturbances not open to members of the monetary union. Some members of the union would regard devaluation by outsiders as a way of exporting unemployment, particularly when unemployment is as high as it has been.

The European Union has discussed this problem but has not found a satisfactory solution. Demanding fixed exchange rates of countries that are not admitted to membership seems an unlikely solution. Failure to find an acceptable solution poses a long-term threat to the trading union if member countries begin to restrict imports from countries that devalue. This risk is not negligible. Increased trade barriers would be a high price to pay for a partial monetary union.

To gain admission to the monetary union, a country is supposed to meet certain criteria for deficits, debt, and inflation. Few countries are likely to meet all the criteria, but the criteria can be waived by a vote of the Council of Ministers. It will be difficult to resolve this problem in a consistent way.

Belgium has a debt ratio of 130 percent of its GDP. It

will not meet the supposed criterion of 60 percent within the lifetime of any living person. Belgium will be admitted, while Portugal, with a debt ratio about half as large, will be excluded.

Far more difficult will be the enforcement of fiscal rules for deficit and debt after a country is admitted to the monetary union. This is a principal point where the economic problem meets the peculiar political structure. The central bank is not part of any government, so governments have incentives to pursue domestic agendas and shift the financing burden to the central bank. Threatening fines for large deficits can work against small countries. But large countries can use their veto power to hamstring the European Union on other issues unrelated to the fiscal problem. Britain recently gave a preview of how such tactics can be used.

In the past fifty years, Western Europe has made remarkable progress developing common institutions to resolve common problems. No one should doubt the importance of this process for greatly reducing the threat of war, expanding opportunities for trade and economic progress, and providing a base for additional institutional development toward a more federal Europe.

Advocates of monetary union claim it is the next important step. They see monetary union as an integrating mechanism that encourages trade expansion and strengthens the economic ties between France and Germany and with other members. At best, the benefits of monetary union will be small, while the risks are large. It seems increasingly likely that part of Europe will join. Let us hope that they will have the good sense to abandon the effort if it proves to be costly and divisive, as I clearly believe it will.

4

The Case for the Euro

Paul Mentré

We are beyond the debate between the skeptics and the true believers on European Monetary Union. The markets, our masters, anticipate the timely implementation of EMU, and a calendar was adopted by the Madrid European Council in December 1995.

If you compare other interest rates with those prevailing for the German Bundesbank, you will note that for France, the Benelux countries, and Austria, the differences in interest rates have shrunk to less than a quarter of a percentage point. In some cases they are even negative. Gradually, this reduction is stretching to short-term maturities.

The increasing credibility of the introduction of the Euro on the financial markets on January 1, 1999, is also demonstrated by the efforts of individual financial actors and of individual financial centers, notably London, Paris, and Frankfurt, to develop strategies to adapt themselves to the new single currency.

In this joint or parallel effort of governments, central banks, and private financial actors, attention has to be paid to the international role of the Euro, to its place in the future international environment.

It is a subject that seems finally to be of interest to Americans. At the G-7 summit in Lyon in the summer of 1996, Secretary Rubin said that he intended to hold further discussions on the matter, which he perceived to be of importance. The theme was again brought back and discussed by him at a 1996 meeting of the G-7 in Washington, D.C.

The Euro in the International Monetary System

To answer the question of what will be the place of the Euro in the international monetary system and in the new international environment, I will start with a description of the likely exchange-rate framework. As far as the Euro zone is concerned, the legal documents that are currently being prepared by the commission will eliminate any ambiguity about the respective role of the Euro and about the national currencies of participating countries. There will be a difference in the expression of the same currency. Financial transactions will be eliminated between the French franc and the deutsche mark. There will be no more quotation in Paris of the dollar versus the French franc or in Frankfurt of the Swiss franc versus the deutsche mark. There will be unified quotations in Frankfurt and in Paris of the Euro against the dollar or the Euro against the Swiss franc.

As far as other European currencies are concerned, progress was made at the Dublin Council of Economic and Finance Ministers at the Dublin summit.

It is clear that high fluctuations of exchange rates between the Euro and the currencies of nonparticipating European countries would impair the functioning of the single market. At the core of the single currency project are two perspectives: a political one, and the idea that a single currency is a necessary complement to the single market. As Mr. Meltzer has pointed out, the evolution of the sterling pound and of the Italian lira after the 1992–1993 crisis was deeply resented in France in terms of competitive advantage.

After the 1996 Dublin Council, one can see what will serve as the framework for intra-European exchange rate relations. There will be bilateral agreements on the volun-

23

tary base. There will be a definition of the exchange rate of individual currencies against the Euro and the acceptance-refusal margins. There will be joint interventions in the market by the European Central Bank and the relevant national central banks, to see to it that the currency remains in the agreed margins.

And there will be a presentation of and an adherence to conversions programs with fiscal discipline consistent with rapid entry of the country, and symmetrically, a possible suspension of interventions if these programs are not respected or if the advice of the European Central Bank and interest rates and exchange rates are not followed by the country.

Since stability of exchange rates during two years will be a precondition for entry at the later stage in the monetary union, this agreement will play an important stabilizing role. With some qualification, it could be extended to future members in time, such as the Eastern European countries.

As far as the relations with other currencies are concerned, one should not expect that a reasonable possibility of exchange rate stability will emerge from the economic and monetary union.

The Maastricht Treaty deals in great detail with the respective role of governments and central banks in the definition and the operation of the international monetary system. But it is quite unlikely that in coming years the definition of such formal agreements covering the international monetary system could take place, in view of the essential role played by short-term capital movements.

It means, then, in the future, the international allocation of assets by private actors, such as institutional investors, will continue to determine external exchange rates of the Euro against other currency.

Let me now describe briefly the likely strategy of financial actors in the various financial centers. The initial concept for the implementation of the Madrid change of scenario was for the Euro to be confined to the financial markets and to the banks, which would continue to have accounts for the customers denominated in national currency and would internally make the necessary conversion. But gradually we have seen the desire of enterprises, and notably the treasurers, to be direct participants in the Euro market. The same is true for institutional investors. Under the pressure of these large customers, banks in all European countries are now preparing for the possibility that the Euro will develop more rapidly in its use by final economic agents than in the Madrid scenario, which had a deadline of 2002.

Competitive Opportunities

European financial actors realize now that the Euro offers a number of major competitive opportunities. For instance, it is now possible to substitute direct banking or direct insurance strategies that would enable actors to commercialize their products in the same currency within the whole of Europe. It means that the place of the Euro in financial assets and debts might prove more significant than many had initially contemplated. In preparation for the emergence of large Euro capital markets, various financial centers in Europe are developing strategies to be ready for the shock of 1999.

As far as Paris is concerned, it has already been announced that as of January 1, 1999, all outstanding public debt, all bond and stock markets, and all futures markets will turn to the Euro in addition to interbank and foreign exchange transactions.

In Germany, similar decisions have been made. Initially, at the time of the Madrid summit, Germany intended to issue its new public securities in Euro, but the conversion of the outstanding debt from the deutsche mark to the Euro, it was said, would take some time. Under pressure of large German banks and institutional investors, however, the German government began to perceive the disadvantages of such a gradual approach.

It would reduce the liquidity of the Euro capital markets, while these markets would have a size which would be smaller than the size of the U.S. Treasury bonds capital markets and, to some extent, fragmented between different national issuers with different ratings.

If financial instruments were to be still denominated in national currencies, some doubts might arise about the stability of the process. Remember that the futures markets in London decided that for maturities extending beyond 1999, contracts will be settled in Euros. They also added that if there were active financial markets in national currencies, they might contemplate reintroducing futures markets in these currencies.

I believe that as of January 1, 1999, the change toward the full integration of the Euro in all segments of the capital markets will effectively take place.

As far as the competition between the financial centers of Europe is concerned, each one wants to stress the advantages it provides. Obviously, the important issue for the United Kingdom is to affirm the place of London as the center of the Euro while having its government, and it seems even its future government, maintaining the option of either joining or not joining the Euro zone at the outset.

If the United Kingdom does not join, there will be associated costs for operations in London, because the London domestic security markets are primarily expressed in sterling and the foreign exchange market is largely dominated by the relationship between the dollar and the Euro.

This is one reason why the Bank of England is so eager to be fully insured: the British banks want to be sure that in any future interbank settlement system in Europe they will not be discriminated against.

The International Allocation of Assets

That leads to my final theme, which is the future of the Euro in its international environs. The financial actors are preparing themselves already for the new dimensions of assets and liabilities management. They will have to ensure that in terms of stocks and of flows, they are fully prepared to monitor the exposure to cover the risk on the Euro-wide scene.

But more fundamentally, for the evolution of the Euro, notably against the dollar, the international allocation of assets by institutional investors will play a key role. Consider, for instance, the attitude of the U.S. or Japanese pension funds, or of the central banks of emerging countries with large reserves, and of mutual funds in all countries.

The role of the international allocation of resources or assets will not be limited to external participants. Institutional investors in Europe themselves will diversify their portfolios in the direction of external holdings. Gradually, we will see the emergence of large, unified, coordinated capital markets getting liquidity in debts comparable with that prevailing on the dollar-dominated capital market.

With markets in Euro-dominated financial instruments largely open to external arbitrators and to internal ones, the evolution of the Euro against the other currencies will be largely dominated by capital flows and by the disciplines of the market itself.

The Fed watchers and the future European Central Bank (ECB) watchers will have to assess monetary policies, the possible evolution, and the likely effect on the respective level of interest rates, which means the difference between long-term interest rates and short-term interest rates, and against medium-term background, which could lead to equalization of real interest rates. One should see, according to these various perceptions and the evolution over time, either cumulative or self-corrective capital movements.

Investors in stocks might want also to have a look at the medium-term economic prospects as far as Europe is concerned. Initially, the ECB will probably want to assert its credibility. That would mean adherence to a strict and nonaccommodating monetary policy that should lead, subject to monetary policies conducted in other countries (notably the United States) to capital flows moving in the direction of the Euro zone.

At the same time, although gradually, investors will see that this exchange rate evolution, combined with a strict monetary policy and the lack of flexibility in policies contained by the stability pact, could well lead to a reduction of the contemplated rate of growth and could thus play a role as a deterrent to investments in European stocks.

There will be two countervailing forces, one of a short-term nature and the other of a medium-term one. We have yet to see the end result of these various forces. In the future, the way in which statistics and economic indicators are interpreted by the various financial actors throughout the world will play a key role in the evolution of the Euro and in the success of our common endeavor to see the unity of Europe realized through the single market, the single currency, and possibly political union.

5
Discussion

MR. ISSING: Mr. Meltzer, you observed that exchange rate movement between the "ins" and the "outs" might endanger the single market. This is one of your arguments against the risks of monetary union.

But this argument has another side, because the existing single market is already endangered by exchange rate movements, as we have seen in the past. Medium-term undervaluations of important currencies raise the question of protectionism in other member countries.

This is an argument you brought forward against a single currency, but it is also an argument in favor of it.

Mr. Mentré, you mentioned that future interest rates for some countries will converge. But for the time being, the interpretation is quite clear. The markets are betting on a political decision. Whatever the economic convergence is, the markets expect that country X and country Y will be accepted.

MR. MELTZER: Yes, there is some risk on both sides. I believe the risk is much greater if you are in a fixed exchange-rate bloc and the others are outside.

The reason for that is, of course, that Europe has previously avoided those problems through periodic revaluations and devaluations of currencies, to realign them. That will become much more difficult once we have the ins and the outs. The ins will have no possibility of realigning their currencies internally. Therefore, the risk will be that countries on the outside—one thinks of Italy and Great Britain, particularly—will pose a real threat to the union. I think they currently pose a great threat to the union, particularly in the French attitude toward the Italian and Spanish devaluations.

MR. ISSING: There is discussion now on European Monetary System II (EMS II), and one of the proposals is that the European Central Bank should have the right to trigger discussions on adjustments of exchange rates to depoliticize this decision. I think this would reduce the danger of misaligned exchanges.

MR. MELTZER: Yes. People are certainly aware of this problem. The question is, can governments achieve a European monetary arrangement under which nonmember countries would have their rates tied to the Euro rate and would be allowed to devalue only with the permission of the European Central Bank?

It is a step in the direction of avoiding this problem. But just as you were unable to keep Exchange Rate Mechanism I (ERM I), it doesn't seem very likely that you are going to be able to keep ERM II. When the pressures build up in a country, as recently in France or Italy or Britain, devaluation is a possibility for governments that are not members of the union.

MR. ISSING: As far as the convergence of interest rates is concerned, the judgment of the market is always a mixture of all the relevant factors, both political and economic. But there is a good sense to economic and financial indicators.

For instance, the spread between the French franc rate and the deutsche mark rate was reduced to nearly zero in the summer of 1996. Because of the deficiencies that were perceived in the drafting of the budget, and the capability of France to adhere to 3 percent, there came a widening of the spreads, notably for short-term maturity. After the presentation of the budget, they came back to the initial June level, which was nearly zero. This means that the markets are reacting to financial indicators.

MR. MENTRÉ: I am sure that the spreads between the French and German rates would have converged anyway, because our politics have converged. We have seen that before Maastricht.

MR. ISSING: Yes. There were concerns that not only political judgment, but the perception of the policies in both countries would determine political decision.

By the way, the reactions of the market will play an important role in the decision to be taken in 1998 on the list of participants, because the governments will act on the proposal of the European Monetary Institute and the commission to create organizations that would have to react to possible disruptions in the markets, if expectations are not fulfilled. This could play a discriminating role in advance of the decision itself.

MR. MELTZER: Mr. Mentré, unemployment in France is now 10.6 percent. It has been above 10 percent now for two years; it is long-term. That is, people do not come into the labor force, drop out, and then come into the labor force again, as they do in the United States. They stay out of the labor force more or less permanently, and this has been going on for a long time.

In response to that, you are taking steps to move toward monetary union. What rate of unemployment do you think is no longer tolerable? Suppose it were to be 15 percent, 18 percent? Is there some rate of unemployment at which you would begin to think that devaluation or some other change of policy would make sense?

Mr. Issing, can the European Monetary Union be made consistent with the social welfare states of Europe, and can both of those be made consistent with sustained economic growth that would raise living standards?

MR. MENTRÉ: I have the answer to Mr. Meltzer's question. Suppose there is a large European country with an unemployment rate of 18 percent, which is firm, and the new prime minister is pushing aggressively to be a member of the Euro zone.

France has had limited structural reforms, but in the right direction. This means that at a given rate of growth there has been a greater rate of employment creation than in the past. If you believe, as I do, that the single currency will provide additional growth to the credibility of a European central bank and the reduction of interest rates associated with it, then you contemplate higher growth. We have to continue to implement structural reforms to connect such growth with a greater content in employment. But *not* to be in the Euro zone would be of no advantage to us.

MR. ISSING: The German welfare system—in the existing form and at the current level—has no chance to survive anyway, with or without monetary union. We have to restructure it. We have to react to the globalization of the world, to what is happening just to the eastern part of Germany. Things are underway. But I am sometimes hopeful, sometimes more pessimistic, that we are on the right track.

But monetary union makes this issue far more complicated, because some supporters of monetary union implicitly give the impression that it would help solve those problems. Of course, monetary union is not a panacea.

If, after entry into monetary union, people find out that labor market problems have become aggravated and more flexibility is needed, they might blame monetary union for disadvantages in the structure of our economies that have nothing to do with monetary union. This is a threat for the political acceptance of the monetary union.

Again, monetary union is not responsible for that, but

the perception is there. There are people who believe that it might be easier to protect the European welfare system behind protectionistic values within the monetary union; in fact, this would be the most dangerous answer to urgent problems.

MR. MENTRÉ: Mr. Issing, how do you see the attitude of the German government as an expression of the German people as far as the conversion of the existing debt to the Euro is concerned?

Mr. Meltzer, I have a question about your judgment on the European Central Bank. When the committee was launched after a fascinating discussion in Rome, it was decided that it would comprise representatives of all European countries—two for the larger ones, one for the smaller ones, as in the EC Commission. Then in a small group we discussed proposals to be made, and a German representative asked me, "Are you ready to accept the independence of the future European Central Bank? If not, there is no point in discussing it, because it cannot fly in Germany."

A key decision in the Maastricht Treaty was independence of the central bank. But personally, I do not see a great difference between the Federal Reserve for Americans and a European Central Bank for Europeans. You said that the Federal Reserve is within the government, but the same is true for the European central banks. The members are designated by the European Council, just as members of the Fed Board are designated by the executive branch in the United States. They have long-term irrevocable terms in both cases, and they make joint decisions with the contributing influences of regional reserve banks. So, what in your judgment are the main differences between the U.S. Fed and the contemplated European Central Bank?

MR. ISSING: Yes, it is true that in Germany, the authorities were reluctant to promise a quick transfer of outstanding public debt into the Euro. That is because our banking structure is marked by a great number of small banks and small investors. This creates complications, because what is now, say, 100,000 deutsche marks will become a very different sum in Euros.

So how should we handle that problem technically? It can be handled, and I think the German banks and German authorities recognize that the liquidity of the market has to be taken into account. We should find a way for the important part of the outstanding public debt to be translated into the Euro from the beginning. Otherwise, the German financial market would suffer.

There is now a debate about how this problem can best be tackled, because it is not necessary that all outstanding debt be converted from the beginning.

MR. MELTZER: Some of the differences are subtle, but they are very important.

First, as William McChesney Martin, one of our longest-standing Federal Reserve governors, used to say, we are independent within the government but we are not independent of the government. That is a big difference, that *in* and *of.*

Here, we have the Humphrey-Hawkins Law. Congress sets the goals for what the central bank can do. Congress can change the goals by legislation, if it wishes.

Second, the Federal Reserve has regulatory authority. It hesitates to give up regulatory authority because it builds a constituency in the banking system for its policy, builds support. Where is the support? The Bundesbank maintains support in a different way, but it is very important. Germans respect the Bundesbank. If the Bundesbank says that the government's policy is wrong, it has a constituency that says that the government's policy is wrong.

The European Central Bank is going to exist without such a constituency and with the added burden that each country that is disadvantaged by it is going to say it is *the*

Bank's fault that *we* have unemployment. It is *their* fault that *we* have these problems with competitive countries. Without such a constituency, it is very difficult to survive.

The Bundesbank and the Swiss national bank, for example, work very hard to maintain that constituency and support within the general population. Without it, they cannot pursue their policies. The European Central Bank, because of the way in which it is structured, does not automatically develop such a constituency. And it develops some hostility, enemies within the ministries of finance, the very first day.

MR. MENTRÉ: I think that the building up of a constituency for the Fed was somewhat similar, because in the monetary history of the United States, you had periods when there was no federal central bank whatsoever. It was created, then abolished, then created again. I think that for Europe and the central bank there will be a gradual building up of a constituency, as well.

And as far as relations with the Congress are concerned, it is provided for in the Maastricht Treaty that governors of the central bank will have to make presentations to parliament.

QUESTION: Whether we like the EMU or not, there are criteria that countries are required to meet to qualify for entry. Is it true that the Czech Republic, if it were a member of the EMU, would meet these criteria and would belong to that very small club who qualified?

PRIME MINISTER KLAUS: Last week we presented to the parliament our eighth budget, and it was the eighth balanced budget. So there is no problem with the budget. We would not be able to meet one of the criteria, because our level of inflation is still higher than the one required by Maastricht criteria. But the Maastricht criteria are missing something, because they do not include criteria like the dynamics of

GDP, industrial growth, growth of wages, and employment level, and those criteria will be relevant when one country is growing much faster than another and the first country is not able to devalue. At that moment, the process of transfers from the more successful to the less successful countries will be an issue.

QUESTION: Prime Minister Klaus, don't you still have exchange controls in the Czech Republic that would not be possible in a common monetary union?

PRIME MINISTER KLAUS: We have a convertibility of currency, and I think that our exchange rate regime is quite liberal. Whether it is absolutely compatible with the ECU, I am not sure—but this is not a real issue. This is something we have time to change. You can decide about exchange controls, whereas to change the rate of inflation or the rate of indebtedness of the country is not a simple decision.

QUESTION: You talked about the core group of countries. The original six are much more homogeneous than are the fifteen all together. Now, the European Monetary Union will probably have a core group that is a bit more homogeneous. Would it be very detrimental for the rest of Europe, be it your country or the ones that belong to the European Union but not the core group yet, if that core group proceeds, and it takes a very long time until other members join?

PRIME MINISTER KLAUS: It seems to me that the European Monetary Union can be introduced. I have no doubt that it can be done. My question is only, At what cost? You are from Germany; you know that the monetary unification of Germany was possible, but the price was enormous.

As minister of finance, I spent several years traveling to Washington, D.C., to get $2.5 billion of credit in the form of various stand-by arrangements for the moment of our radical move to price liberalization in the deregulation of foreign trade. This $2.5 billion represented a credit to be repaid, and it cost several years of my activity and the activity of my colleagues. East Germany was probably getting billions of dollars a week in the past five years, and not as a credit, but as a gift. Monetary unification can be accomplished. But is the solidarity among the European countries as authentic as the solidarity between West Germany and East Germany? That is my only question, and I am afraid that the answer is not so clearly explained to the taxpayers in many European countries. But definitely, it can be done, with five countries, eight countries, ten countries, twenty countries—it is only a matter of the price being higher.

But some countries, including the Netherlands, Austria, and Germany, have been members of an implicit monetary union for the past fifteen years. There are countries that can do this without any problem.

QUESTION: Prime Minister, can there be a monetary union without some significant transfer of fiscal responsibilities to Brussels or to some central group? And will that, in fact, inevitably transfer political power from the countries in a more homogeneous or a more centralized Europe?

PRIME MINISTER KLAUS: I am sure that a transfer of money from various countries to Brussels means the transfer of political power, by definition. The transfer is inevitable, and a transfer of political power is, therefore, inevitable.

QUESTION: There was an advertisement in one of the IMF papers today by Kommerzbank that said, "The Euro, serious competition for the dollar." In effect, it was elaborating on the point that Mr. Mentré made earlier, that as the capital markets expand and there is more liquidity, more depth, and more breadth, foreign savings will come in. This will make the Euro a very strong currency. I assume here that the central bank will be very tough on inflation for some time. This will put upward pressure on the Euro and will probably weaken the trade balance in the current account. Potentially it will increase unemployment and slow the growth rate within Europe. Do you anticipate a greater increase in unemployment coming after the adjustment in the fiscal positions?

I have one other question, also. Suppose that the G-7 peg their exchange rates: that is, that the Euro and the dollar and the deutsche mark and the yen are to be kept within some designated range. They have done this before. What happens if there is a conflict between that objective, as set by the governments or by finance ministers, and the objective of achieving price stability on the part of the European Monetary Union?

MR. ISSING: Indeed, it concerns me that there are contradictory promises for the Euro. On the one hand, it is said that it will be a stable currency, as stable as the deutsche mark, or even more stable. It will be a currency creating competition for the U.S. dollar, and that has the consequences you described. On the other hand, exporters in Germany have the impression that they have fewer exchange rate worries than in the past.

I am strictly opposed to a target zone system's being established for the dollar, the yen, and the Euro, especially for the first years of the Euro. That will be a period of extreme change, and investors' and authorities' behavior will be uncertain. What we will need is a flexibility of exchange rate between those currency zones. Fixing the rates would only increase the burden for achieving sound monetary policy in Europe.

The Maastricht Treaty contains a clause stating that any exchange-rate arrangement made by the states should not be in conflict with the goal of price stability. Whether this is much help, we will have to see. I think we should avoid fixing parities among those three currencies.

MR. MENTRÉ: The French tradition has favored stability and the target zone system, but I personally agree with Mr. Issing that the likelihood of such a system being put in place in the first years of the Euro is minimal.

QUESTION: Mr. Mentré made the point, quite rightly, in my view, that the policy debate in Europe is largely over, and the players are increasingly acting on the assumption that this will happen on the first of January, 1999. Mr. Issing made the point that the Bundesbank is actively preparing. To my mind, Mr. Meltzer made one of the most persuasive arguments in favor of EMU in his early comments, that Europe has much greater priorities. Europe must reform the cap, it must cope with enlargement to the east, it must reform its institutions. Europe can do none of these things without political cohesion, and all these things are interconnected. There is no unraveling these elements from one another; they must all happen together. At this stage, all the governments are committed in the direction of the EMU; the players are committed and investing in the likelihood that EMU is going to take place. Political credibility is at stake in favor of this event happening. How could the failure of the EMU to take place fail to unravel the political unity that has been built up over the past forty-five years? How can there be any other cause than to move forward with this next step toward political integration?

MR. MELTZER: In NATO, we managed to put together political arrangements independently of having a federal structure or a common monetary union. In the World Trade Organization, we put together a trading organization without having a political structure. In the Rio conventions, we managed to put together some pollution controls without a political structure. We don't need these political structures.

I think the Europeans are selling themselves on the idea that monetary union is an important forward political step. It seems to me that it is not. It is going to be a source of continuing problems for Europe. If there were really an effort to deal with the political union, which I very much would like to see, then they ought to address those questions and leave monetary union aside. Monetary union is not going to be resolved on January 1, 1999, or even in 2002. It is going to be a continuing set of issues and possibly a crisis.

QUESTION: Of course there are costs, there are risks. But there have been costs and risks in every step ever taken. The mold has to be broken. Europe cannot break the mold without embarking on costs, without entailing some risks. Those decisions have been made.

MR. MELTZER: I have very little doubt that they will go ahead on January 1, 1999, and I have said nothing to the contrary. My question is, Will they still be there in 2001?

QUESTION: As I listen to the discussion here, I am thinking about the roles of money, and it raises an interesting question. Certainly, the Euro will be established as a unit of account and as a medium of exchange. As one who thinks intensely about the best ways to store wealth, I wonder about the store of value role. If I want to store large amounts of wealth over time, I can choose from among several alternatives. The deutsche mark is going to go away pretty soon. I can choose to store in Japanese yen, I can choose to store in U.S. dollars, and I can choose to store in Swiss francs.

The prospective Euro is somewhat problematic. It will be a new currency. We don't know who the participants will be. So if you are asking me to store wealth between now and the year 2006, I'm a little nervous about storing it in Euros, because I don't know whether it will be the currency of only the core European countries, with their professed adherence to fiscal discipline, or if it will include Spain and Italy, or if it will include some other countries that might eventually qualify.

So I suggest that as we move toward currency union, the store of value properties of the Euro, which ultimately are the only enduring properties of a currency, will have to be defined. Here again, we are playing an interesting game, and the political leaders in charge of the evolution of the Euro have to be very careful about defining what the Euro is going to be fairly soon.

If not, then I expect that we will see more of what has begun in Europe. A great many automobiles with French and German license plates are driving into Switzerland, because they are looking for a way to store wealth and the Swiss franc looks a bit safer than the Euro right now.

Another possibility would be a desire to store wealth in yen—or maybe even in dollars.

DATE DUE

GAYLORD

PRINTED IN U.S.A.